# CELEBRATING THE CITY OF SYDNEY

# Celebrating the City of Sydney

Walter the Educator

Silent King Books

**SILENT KING BOOKS**

# SKB

Copyright © 2024 by Walter the Educator

All rights reserved. No part of this book may be reproduced in any manner whatsoever without written permission except in the case of brief quotations embodied in critical articles and reviews.

First Printing, 2024

Disclaimer
This book is a literary work; the story is not about specific persons, locations, situations, and/or circumstances unless mentioned in a historical context. Any resemblance to real persons, locations, situations, and/or circumstances is coincidental. This book is for entertainment and informational purposes only. The author and publisher offer this information without warranties expressed or implied. No matter the grounds, neither the author nor the publisher will be accountable for any losses, injuries, or other damages caused by the reader's use of this book. The use of this book acknowledges an understanding and acceptance of this disclaimer.

Celebrating the City of Sydney is a little collectible souvenir book that belongs to the Celebrating Cities Book Series by Walter the Educator. Collect them all and more books at WaltertheEducator.com

USE THE EXTRA SPACE TO TAKE NOTES AND DOCUMENT YOUR MEMORIES

# SYDNEY

In the dawn's tender light, where dreams and sea meet,

# Celebrating the City of
# Sydney

Sydney awakens, her heart a rhythmic beat.

Sunrise crowns her, a diadem of gold,

A tale of epochs in her whispers told.

Emerald waves caress her shores so grand,

Nature's art in every grain of sand.

Opera House sails, a swan in flight,

Glistening pearl under moon's soft light.

Bridges like outstretched arms embrace,

Steel and grace in a timeless race.

# Celebrating the City of Sydney

Harbour, a mirror of sky's endless hue,

Reflecting the cosmos, both old and new.

In the Rocks, history's echoes reside,

Cobblestones whisper of time's gentle glide.

Convict past and dreams anew,

Mingling stories of many a crew.

Botanical gardens, a verdant embrace,

Nature's hymn in every space.

# Celebrating the City of Sydney

Waratahs and wattle in a fragrant dance,

Inviting all into a trance.

Skyscrapers kiss the heavens above,

Concrete and glass with the city's love.

Modernity's pulse in each design,

Blending with past, a seamless line.

Circular Quay, where stories converge,

Ferries glide, a gentle surge.

Tourists marvel at the panoramic feast,

A canvas where East melds with the West.

Coogee to Bondi, a coastal trail,

Cliffs and waves tell a vibrant tale.

Surfers conquer the ocean's roar,

In a dance that's ancient lore.

Darling Harbour, alive with cheer,

Laughter and joy fill the air.

Aquarium's depths and wildlife bright,

A city's heart in sheer delight.

Markets bustling with eclectic wares,

Artisans share their crafted cares.

Spices mingle in the evening air,

cultures rare.

Ode to Sydney, a city so grand,

Her beauty crafted by nature's hand.

In her embrace, a world's delight,

A beacon shining through day and night.

# Celebrating the City of Sydney

# ABOUT THE CREATOR

Walter the Educator is one of the pseudonyms for Walter Anderson. Formally educated in Chemistry, Business, and Education, he is an educator, an author, a diverse entrepreneur, and he is the son of a disabled war veteran. "Walter the Educator" shares his time between educating and creating. He holds interests and owns several creative projects that entertain, enlighten, enhance, and educate, hoping to inspire and motivate you. Follow, find new works, and stay up to date with
Walter the Educator™ at
WaltertheEducator.com.

www.ingramcontent.com/pod-product-compliance
Lightning Source LLC
LaVergne TN
LVHW012048070526
838201LV00082B/3861